I WILL SHINE BRIGHT

WRITTEN BY
MALASHIA LARAE

ILLUSTRATED BY
PIGGIE ILLUSTRATORS

Copyright © 2023 by Malashia Croom

All rights reserved. No part of this book may be reproduced or used in any manner without written permission of the copyright owner except for the use of quotations in a book review.

First Printing edition April 2023

Book design by Piggie Illustrators
Author by Malashia Croom

ISBN: 979-8-218-19224-2 (paperback)

Published and Printed by lulu.com

I SHINE BRIGHT LIKE A STAR AND I'M HAPPY TO BE IN MY OWN SKIN.

LIKE BAD WEATHER, HOLD MY HAND, AND WE CAN RUN THROUGH THE RAIN TOGETHER.

LIKE A GAME IN BASKETBALL, WE WILL NOT BE ROUGH, PUSH OR SHOVE. WE'LL ALL SHARE, BE FAIR AND PLAY THE GAME WITH LOVE.

BRIGHT GIRLS, LET YOUR HAIR DOWN, EMBRACE YOUR SKIN AND BEAUTIFUL CURLS, LIKE ART, WE ARE PAINTED WITH ALL DIFFERENT COLORS IN THE WORLD.

LIKE CRAYONS, WE ALL DRAW AND CREATE PICTURES THE SAME. WE ARE ALL EQUAL, AND WILL HONOR EACH OTHER'S ACHIEVEMENTS AND GOALS LIKE THE HALL OF FAME.

LIKE THE BLUE OCEAN, WE LEARN TO SWIM AND BE BRAVE ENOUGH TO STAY AFLOAT. LIKE A CAPTAIN ON A SHIP, WE WORK TOGETHER TO PADDLE AND LEAD THE BOAT.

THE AUTHORS PURPOSE:

MY HOPES AND PURPOSE OF THIS STORY IS TO SHED LIGHT OF ALL RACES, RELIGIONS, AGES, APPEARANCE, DIVERSITY AND MANY MORE OF THE STEREOTYPE CHALLENGES CHILDREN FACE TODAY. THE CONCEPT OF THE STORY IS TO REFLECT AND HELP REDUCE LESS EXPERIENCES OF CHILDREN BEING JUDGED, BIASED OR PREJUDICE TOWARDS ONE ANOTHER. INSTEAD, INCREASE CHILDREN'S CONFIDENCE AND BUILD POWERFUL FRIENDSHIPS WITHIN THE COMMUNITY WE ALL SHARE ALONG WITH LEARNING ONE ANOTHER'S ETHICAL BACKGROUND. WITH ANOTHER GOAL OF BRINGING CHILDREN CLOSER TOGETHER AND CREATING A SAFE ENVIRONMENT WHERE THEY CAN TRULY BE THEMSELVES WITHOUT FEAR.

WHY READ US?

AT TIMES OTHER CHILDREN MAY SEE OTHER CHILDREN DIFFERENTLY BASED ON HOW THEY LOOK OR SPEAK. HOWEVER, TEACHING THE IMPORTANCE OF DIVERSITY AND WHAT THE MEANING OF " THE MELTING POT" REALLY REPLICATES. IN TODAY'S SOCIETY, CHILDREN SHOULD ULTIMATELY BRING NEW IDEA'S AND EXPERIENCES WHERE CHILDREN CAN LEARN AND GROW FROM EACH OTHER. DIFFERENT IDEAS AND PERSPECTIVES LEAD TO BETTER PROBLEM- SOLVING WHICH WILL TRULY CREATE THE REAL CORE VALUE OF WHAT DIVERSITY STANDS FOR AND FEELING EQUAL. MY PURPOSE IS TO ALWAYS BELIEVE IN EQUALITY AMONGST COLOR AND MANY OTHER CHALLENGES WITHIN RACE TO TEACH ALL OF THE YOUNG GIRLS AND BOYS IN THE WORLD THAT THEIR VOICE WILL ALWAYS MATTER AND HOW POWERFUL CHILDREN ARE UNITED AS ONE. NO RACE SHOULD FEEL SUPERIOR THAN THE OTHER AND WE MUST INSTALL THIS CONCEPT IN CHILDREN. THIS STORY WAS MADE WITH A SIGNIFICANT AMOUNT OF COMPASSION AND LOVE. IN HOPES OF CREATING A STRONG PURPOSE TO MAKE THE WORLD A SAFER ENVIRONMENT STARTING WITH EDUCATING OUR CHILDREN WITH HOW BRIGHT AND BRILLIANT THEY ARE TO OUR WORLD, NO MATTER WHO THEY ARE OR WHERE THEY COME FROM. EQUALITY TRULY STARTS WITHIN OUR OWN FOUNDATION. SPREAD LOVE AND PEACE.

www.ingramcontent.com/pod-product-compliance
Lightning Source LLC
Chambersburg PA
CBHW042036150426
43194CB00032B/132